TUBE STATION FACTFILE

BY

COLIN PITT

ISBN 978-1-910241-87-5

Publishing by CP Press 2019

CONTENTS

BAKERLOO LINE

Created in 1906 its full name was the Baker Street & Waterloo Railway. At one time the line used to go further north than just to Harrow & Wealdstone. It went to Watford Junction.

Elephant & Castle

At Elephant & Castle the tunnels continue South for several hundred yards as at one time extension to Camberwell had been planned.

There are two emergency staircases at Elephant & Castle, one for the Bakerloo line and one for the Northern line

Lambeth North

Lambeth North opened as Kennington Road in March 1906 and became Westminster Bridge Road in August 1906 and then became known as Lambeth (North) in 1917.

Waterloo

When the line was first proposed this would have been the southern terminus.

Charing Cross

Platform walls are decorated with copies of works of art on display in the National Gallery.

This entrance is the one nearest to Barry's Charing Cross Hotel (now the Amba Hotel) of 1864.

Piccadilly Circus

First underground station to be fitted with fluorescent lighting in October 1945.

Oxford Circus

The busiest station on the Underground system, there are two station frontages one built for what is today's Central line in 1900 on the east side of Argyle Street and the other built on the west side for the Bakerloo line in 1906.

Regent's Park

Like Warwick Avenue this is another Bakerloo line station with no surface building.

Baker Street

Baker Street has ten platforms and platforms 5 and 6 served the very first section of the Underground when it opening in January 1863. It has the most platforms of any Underground station.

On the Circle and Hammersmith & City lines Baker Street is between Great Portland Street and Edgware Road.

On the Metropolitan line Baker Street is between Great Portland Street and Finchley Road.

On the Bakerloo line Baker Street is between Regent's Park and Marylebone.

On the Jubilee line Baker Street is between Bond Street and St. John's Wood.

Tiles on some platforms at Baker Street depict Sherlock Holmes smoking his trademark pipe.

Marylebone

At the end of the platform there is a clue as to the original name of the station, with the words 'GREAT CENTRAL' in the tiling.

Edgware Road

Edgware Road has grass growing on its south wall that faces the A40. The station was restored in the 1990's with new tiling in the original style.

Paddington

The tiles along the platform level depict men working in a tunnelling shield and digging the Tube tunnels.

Paddington along with Edgware Road and Hammersmith has the same name for two stations.

Warwick Avenue

Warwick Avenue is unusual for a Bakerloo line station in that it does not have a surface level building.

Maida Vale

Maida Vale was staffed entirely by women when it opened during the First World War in 1915.

Kilburn Park

Kilburn Park has great green and white tiles in the ticket hall area.

The exterior of Kilburn Park Station is one of the last terra-cotta-tiled frontages to be built for the Underground.

Queens Park and Kensal Green

Passengers on Bakerloo line trains travel through a train depot between Queen's Park and Kensal Green.

Willesden Junction

The station has 'high level' and 'low level' platforms used mainly by London Overground. Lower level tracks and shared with Bakerloo line services.

Harlesden to Kenton

All of these stations are owned by Network Rail, but managed by the Underground.

Harrow & Wealdstone

For many years Bakerloo line trains went right up to Watford Junction but since 1982 Harrow & Wealdstone is as far as they go.

Harrow & Wealdstone was the scene of a major main line train crash on 8 October 1952.

CENTRAL LINE

The Central line started in 1900 when it opened as the Central London Railway. It first operated from Shepherd's Bush to Bank. It expanded to West Ruislip in the west. In the east it once reached Ongar but now only goes as far as Epping.

Epping

Epping has one of the largest car parks anywhere on the Underground. Trains used to go further up the line to Ongar.

Since 1994 trains only go as far as Ongar.

Theydon Bois

The old stationmaster's cottage still survives adjacent to the modern-day entrance.

Debden

In an adjacent building Bank of England banknotes are printed.

Loughton

Architect of Loughton Station was John Murrey Easton.

This is the third Loughton station to have existed since the town was first served by the railway in 1865. The station opened for suburban steam train services in 1940 and was transferred to the Underground with the introduction of the electrified Central line.

Buckhurst Hill

This part of the Central line uses parts of what used to be the steam-operated Eastern Counties Railway.

Woodford

Here the line branches off to Roding Valley and Hainault as well as going on to Epping.

South Woodford

There is an 1856 station building on the eastbound side from before it became part of the underground.

Snaresbrook

Canopies on the platforms here have attractive metal brackets.

Roding Valley

This is one of the least used stations on the Underground.

Chigwell

At Chigwell on the Hainault Loop most trains terminate at Woodford, but a few carry on through to Central London.

Grange Hill

The box-shaped ticket hall replaced the original station building here in 1948.

Hainault

The large train depot to the north of the station was used by the U.S. Army during the Second World War.

Fairlop

An RAF airfield was built on Fairlop Plain in 1940 and it was once planned as the site of a new London airport before Heathrow was chosen.

Barkingside

On the southbound platform the waiting room is an original Great Eastern Railway building from over one hundred years ago.

Newbury Park

Exit the station and you find yourself in a bus station under a large concrete canopy. It is now Grade II listed.

Gants Hill

Gants Hill station which opened in 1947 was one of the last three designs for the Underground by architect Charles Holden.

Platforms at Gants Hill have gorgeous uplighters.

Gants Hill is based upon designs for the Moscow subway network.

Redbridge

Sections of the Central line between Gants Hill and Wanstead were used during the Second World War to build aeroplane parts.

Wanstead

Wanstead station was the last major work for the underground by architects Adams, Holden & Pearson.

Leytonstone

Leytonstone station has a series of wall mosaics that commemorate the work of film director Alfred Hitchcock.

Alfred Hitchcock was born locally to Leytonstone in 1899.

Leyton

The facade here hides an earlier building that existed when the original steam-operated line was taken over from the LNER.

Stratford

The westbound Central line is one of two points on the network where doors open on both sides of the platform. The other is Barking.

Mile End

Mile End station has cross-platform interchange below ground between Underground trains of two different sizes. Here District line sub-surface trains meet the Central line tube trains on the same level.

Bethnal Green

The clocks on the platforms here have roundels used on the faces instead of numerals.

Bank

The station suffered a direct hit by a bomb in the 1940 Blitz.

At one time one of the entrances to Bank Underground Station was in the crypt of St. Mary Woolnoth church. It can be seen here but is no longer used. Bank Station's ticket hall had been constructed underneath the church.

St. Pauls

St. Pauls station was orginally named Post Office from 1900 to 1937.

Chancery Lane

This is the only station on the Central line with a Second World War deep level shelter built beneath it.

Holborn

From Holborn to Tottenham Court Road looking out of the windows you may see remains of British Museum station.

British Museum opened on 30th July 1900 and closed on 24th September 1933.

Tottenham Court Road

In 1986 this station received very expensive platform décor by artist Eduardo Paolozzi.

The intricate patterns on the mosaic tiles represented what was then the local hi-fi industry.

Tottenham Court Road station has been the subject of a massive redevelopment. The spacious new main ticket hall is decorated by a "Diamonds and Circles" theme created by French artist Daniel Buren.

Oxford Circus

Oxford Circus is the third busiest station on the network. There are two station frontages. One was built on the east side of Argyll Street for today's Central line in 1900 and another on the west side of Argyll street for the Bakerloo line in 1906.

Bond Street

A new entrance and new lifts were installed at this station in 2017 when it was upgraded.

Marble Arch

The station was opened on 30 July 1900 by the Central London Railway and is between Lancaster Gate and Bond Street stations on the Central line.

Lancaster Gate

Like Marble Arch, Lancaster Gate also opened on 30 July 1900. The original station building was by the line's architect Harry Bell Measures but it was demolished as part of a re-development in 1968. The station was refurbished in 2016.

Queensway

Queensway tube station opened on 30 July 1900 as Queen's Road. It was renamed Queensway on 1 September 1946. The building is a rare survivor of the buildings designed for the Central London Railway by Harry Bell Measures.

Notting Hill Gate

The station was rebuilt in the late 1950's and re-opened on 1 March 1959 linking two Notting Hill Gate's stations on the Circle and District and Central lines.

Holland Park

The station closed for refurbishment in January 2016 re-opening later in the year. Prior to the refurbishment it was one of the 37 last deep level underground stations to retain the original 1950's signage.

Shepherd's Bush

The original station opened on 30th July 1900 and was the original western terminus of the Central London Railway. The station was closed for eight months in 2008 while the original surface station building was replaced with a completely new structure.

White City

White City is one of only a few 'right-hand running' stations, meaning that the trains are on the wrong side to what you would expect.

East Acton

The platforms here have wooden waiting shelters painted in Great Western Railway colours. However they are modern replacements.

North Acton

There is a once-a-day Chiltern Railways 'Parliamentary Train' service that runs along this section of line.

West Acton

West Acton is a Grade II listed station and was built in 1948 for London Transport by the Great Western Railway.

Ealing Broadway

Built by the Great Western Railway for Central line trains in 1920.

Hanger Lane

This round station is in the middle of a roundabout with a network of subway tunnels leading to it.

Perivale

Perivale is another Grade II listed building and was also designed and built by the Great Western Railway.

Greenford

Diesel trains on a service from West Ealing connect with Underground trains here.

Northolt

Along this part of the Central line runs the 'New North Main line' and this runs from Paddington to West Ruislip and beyond.

South Ruislip

The drum-shaped station building was completed in 1960.

Ruislip Gardens

Until 1958 there were British Rail platforms here too. They were accessed through a subway from the ticket hall.

West Ruislip

In the 1930's when the Central line was being extended two more stations - Harefield Road and Denham - were planned but never got built.

There are five 'Ruislip' stations. They are Ruislip, Ruislip Gardens, Ruislip Manor, South Ruislip and West Ruislip.

At West Ruislip this is where London Underground tracks would have carried on had the planned Harefield Road and Denham stations been built.

CIRCLE AND HAMMERSMITH & CITY LINES

The Circle line was born out of two competing Underground railway companies - The Metropolitan and Metropolitan District. They formed 'The Inner Circle' in 1884.

The Hammersmith & City line was a part of the Metropolitan line until being given its own identity in 1990.

Edgware Road

On the outside of the building is the lettering 'Metropolitan Railway' for whom the station was re-built in the 1920's.

Edgware Road, along with Hammersmith and Paddington has two separate stations with the same name.

Edgware Road and Baker Street were both parts of the original stretch of the Underground that opened in 1863.

Baker Street

There is a war memorial and WW1 shell between platforms 2 and 5.

Great Portland Street

Here the lights hanging from the ceiling give an atmospheric feel to the station platforms.

Euston Square

Along the platform are yellow and purple roundels that are solid in colour with the name of the lines that Euston Square services.

King's Cross St. Pancras

King's Cross has the greatest number of Underground lines of any station. It is the busiest Underground station.

Farringdon

At Farringdon the frieze below the roof shows the station's name at the time: Farringdon & High Holborn.

Barbican

The station opened with the name Aldersgate Street on 23 December 1865. The station's name was shortened to Aldersgate on 1 November 1910 and was then again renamed on 24 October 1924 as Aldersgate & Barbican. From 1 December 1968 it has been know as just Barbican.

Moorgate

The station was opened as Moorgate Street in 1865 by the Metropolitan Railway. In 1900 the City & South London Railway added the station to its network. The Great Northern & City Railway began serving the station in 1904.

Liverpool Street

Liverpool Street was built as a dual-level station with provision for the Underground. It is served by the Central line, Circle line, Hammersmith & City line and the Metropolitan line. It is the sixth busiest Underground station and was originally named Bishopsgate before being renamed Liverpool Street on 1 November 1909.

Aldgate

Aldgate was opened on 18 November 1876 with its entrance on Aldgate High Street. Services from Aldgate originally ran further west going as far as Richmond at one time.

Tower Hill

There was another Tower Hill Station that existed nearby until 1967. It was originally known as Mark Lane station and opened on 6 October 1884.

Monument

Monument Station is named after the Monument to the Great Fire of London. Monument station opened with the name Eastcheap on 6 October 1884 and was renamed "The Monument" on 1 November 1884.

Cannon Street

On 6 October 1884 the final section of the Inner Circle (now the Circle line) was opened along with Cannon Street station.

Mansion House

Despite its name it is not the nearest tube station to Mansion House itself. That is directly opposite an entrance to Bank station. The station was opened on 3 July 1871 by the Metropolitan District Railway.

Blackfriars

The Underground station pre-dates the mainline one being opened on 30 May 1870. Blackfriars station was significantly renovated between 2009 and 2012.

Temple

Temple station was opened on 30 May 1870 by the District Railway and originally had the name "The Temple".

Embankment

Embankment station is served by the Circle, District, Northern and Bakerloo lines.

It has sub-surface platforms opened in 1870 by the District Railway and deep-level platforms opened in 1906 by the Baker Street and Waterloo Railway and deep-level platforms opened in 1914 by the Charing Cross, Euston and Hampstead Railway.

Westminster

From Westminster underground station it is possible to get into the House of Commons directly from the Underground station. The secret entrance is for Members of Parliament only.

St. James' Park

The headquarters of London Underground are above the station here at 55 Broadway. The building was designed by Charles Holden, and there are sculptures by Jacob Epstein and Eric Gill.

Sloane Square

The large metal pipe that runs across the station at the western end is the river Westbourne, which is diverted and encased at this point.

South Kensington

Turn right after exiting the ticket barriers and you will see the subway that connects the station with South Kensington's museums it is one of the longest subways to an Underground station.

Like Gloucester Road, South Kensington uses the old District Railway building for the entrance and exit.

Gloucester Road

The original Piccadilly line station building abuts the earlier Metropolitan District Railway station.

High Street Kensington

The station is between Gloucester Road and Notting Hill Gate on the Circle line and between Earl's Court and Notting Hill Gate on the District line.

The station has four platforms and platforms 3 and 4 are used for terminating District line trains from Earl's Court.

Notting Hill Gate

Circle and District line platforms were opened on 1 October 1868 by the Metropolitan Railway while Central line platforms were opened on 30 July 1900 by the Central London Railway.

Bayswater

When the Circle line was constructed in the late 1860's it was necessary to demolish two houses in Leinster Gardens, Bayswater. To avoid leaving a gap replica facades that were five feet deep were built. Numbers 23 and 24 Leinster Gardens are dummy homes.

Inside Bayswater Underground station.

Paddington

There are two Paddington stations. This one is on Praed Street and there is a nice red iron footbridge across the tracks.

Royal Oak

Royal Oak like Angel, Elephant & Castle, Manor House and Swiss Cottage is named after a pub.

Westbourne Park

Westbourne Park appears in the 1980's pop video for Boris Gardener's "I want to wake up with you."

Ladbroke Grove

Opened by the Hammersmith and City Railway on 13 June 1864 the station was originally named Notting Hill. It was renamed Notting Hill & Ladbroke Grove in 1880 and Ladbroke Grove (North Kensington) on 1 June 1919. It acquired its present name in 1938. It is the nearest to Portobello Road Market.

Latimer Road

The station opened on 16 December 1868. It is on the Circle and Hammersmith & City line between Wood Lane and Ladbroke Grove stations.

Wood Lane

Wood Lane station was designed by Ian Ritchie Architects and has a 25 metre-high glass screen facade.

Shepherd's Bush Market

It was in 2008 that the new London Overground Shepherd's Bush railway station opened and to avoid confusion the Hammersmith & City line station was renamed Shepherd's Bush Market on 12 October 2008.

Goldhawk Road

The O2 Shepherd's Bush Empire, designed by Frank Matcham, is a short walk from Goldhawk Road station.

Hammersmith

This is the other Hammersmith station to the one over the road that serves the District and Piccadilly lines.

DISTRICT LINE

The District line came from what was originally called the Metropolitan District Railway.

Ealing Broadway

Here at the end of the line the platforms have replicas of 100 year old signs with solid red discs.

Ealing Common

There is a seven-pointed-star in the floor tiles of the ticketing area at this station.

Acton Town

Acton has four platforms. The inside ones are used by the Piccadilly line and the outside ones are usually used by District line Trains.

EALING BROADWAY

EALING BROADWAY
or somebody
else will

Chiswick Park

Chiswick Park station is by architect Charles Holden. The ticket hall is a double height brick drum with a single central column. A brick tower marks the station from a distance.

Turnham Green

A couple of minutes walk from the station is St. Michael and All Angels church, by architect Richard Norman Shaw.

Stamford Brook

In January 1964 Stamford Brook was the station where automatic ticket gates were first trialled.

Ravenscourt Park

Ravenscourt Park station was opened as Shaftesbury Road by the London and South Western Railway on 1 January 1869. On 1 March 1888 the station was given the name Ravenscourt Park.

Gunnersbury

The London Overground service joins the District line here for the service to Richmond.

Kew Gardens

At one time you could have walked from the pub on the eastbound platform straight onto the platform.

The footbridge to the south of the station is Grade II listed.

Richmond

The station is managed by the South Western Railway and the station building was designed by James Robb Scott.

The station has seven platforms with Platforms 1 and 2 for South Western Railway services and Platforms 5, 6 and 7 normally used for District line services.

West Kensington

The station was opened by the District Railway on 9 September 1874 as 'North End (Fulham). It was renamed West Kensington in 1877.

Earl's Court

On 4 October 1911 the first escalators on the Underground opened at Earl's Court. Nowadays the longest escalator on the Underground is at Angel and the shortest escalator is at Stratford.

View of Earl's Court station.

Kensington (Olympia)

The station is unique in that it has a regular service only at weekends.

West Brompton

Since 2000 West Brompton station has been a Grade II Listed Building.

Fulham Broadway

The station was opened as Walham Green on 1 March 1880 when the District Railway extended its line from West Brompton to Putney Bridge. The name was changed to Fulham Broadway on 1 March 1952. Walking out of the station and turning right you will find the entrance building of the old station.

Inside the old Fulham Broadway station which is now an indoor market where you can eat and drink. There are design features from the Underground still evident.

Parsons Green

Parsons Green station was designed under the supervision of John Wolfe-Barry and was opened on 1 March 1880 by the Metropolitan District Railway.

Putney Bridge

Putney Bridge has some unusual roundels on the westbound platforms with a thin red edge.

East Putney

Trains from the South Western Railway sometimes pass through here to go to and from the depot at Wimbledon Park.

Southfields

When the Wimbledon tennis championships are on the platforms of this station are often covered with imitation grass.

Wimbledon Park

This station and neighbouring Southfields were built in 1889.

Wimbledon

Along with Richmond this station is operated by South Western Railways.

Aldgate East

Aldgate East station is not where it was when the line was built, the original 1884 station was moved in 1938.

Whitechapel

Whitechapel station is served by both London Overground and London Underground. The station is unique in that the London Overground service here passes under the Underground.

Stepney Green

On the way into the station is a very old style sign saying 'To The Trains' with a hand and finger graphic.

Bow Road/Bromley-by-Bow

This section of the underground has one of the steepest gradients.

West Ham

West Ham station is also served by c2c into Fenchurch Street, the Jubilee line and the Docklands Light Railway.

Plaistow

At Plaistow Underground you can see an old 'Ticket Office' sign.

Upton Park

The station was opened by the London, Tilbury and Southend Railway in 1877. District line service began in 1902.

East Ham

The station has two platforms and much of the Victorian station once connected to the Tottenham and Forest Gate Railway until 1958.

Barking

Here the subways have long sloping ramps and at this station Eastbound District line trains open their doors on both sides

Upney and Becontree

British Railways used to stop services here but ceased in 1962.

Dagenham Heathway

The station opened in 1932 and initially was operated by the London, Midland and Scottish Railway. The station was called Heathway when it first opened becoming Dagenham Heathway in 1949.

Dagenham East

The station was initially opened as a mainline station in 1885 on the London, Tilbury and Southend Railway.

Elm Park

The station opened in 1935 with the District Railway having been incorporated into London Transport in 1933.

Hornchurch

Another station originally opened on 1 May 1885 by the London, Tilbury and Southend Railway. The station was completely rebuilt in 1932 by the London, Midland and Scottish Railway and an additional pair of platforms constructed to serve the electric District Railway.

Upminster Bridge

Upminster Bridge station was constructed by the London Midland & Scottish Railway for District line train services in 1934. The station building is polygon-shaped and the octagonal tile feature reflects a similar shaped roof light.

Upminster

Upminster is another of a small number of stations on the Underground not owned or managed by TFL.

JUBILEE LINE

The Jubilee line was going to be called 'The Fleet line' but was called The Jubilee line to mark the Queen's Jubilee in 1977. However it ended up opening two years later in 1979.

Stanmore

Stanmore station was opened on 10 December 1932 by the Metropolitan Railway. The station's building and those on the branch were designed by the Metropolitan Railway's architect Charles W. Clarke.

Canons Park

This station was also opened on 10 December 1932 and is between Stanmore and Queensbury stations on the Jubilee line.

Queensbury and Kingsbury

Kingsbury station opened on 10 December 1932 while Queensbury station opened on 16 December 1934 and both were part of the Metropolitan line and were transferred to the Bakerloo line in 1939 and then the Jubilee line in 1979.

Neasden, Dollis Hill, Willesden Green and Kilburn.

All the stations on this stretch of the Jubilee line run alongside the Metropolitan line so some stations have disused platforms each side.

At Kilburn there is a nice bridge outside the station with the name 'METROPOLITAN RAILWAY' along it.

The main station buildings are examples of the work of Charles Walter Clark, the Metropolitan Railway's architect. Willesden Green station opened on 24 November 1879 and was renamed Willesden Green and Cricklewood on 1 June 1894.

The ticket hall interior retains much of the original green tesserae mosaic tiling. Willesden Green station was given Grade II Listed Building status in December 2006.

West Hampstead

West Hampstead has three railway stations serving different lines.

Swiss Cottage

The station was opened on 20 November 1939 when the Metropolitan line's services were transferred to the Bakerloo line. It is named after a nearby pub. The Bakerloo line station was later transferred to the Jubilee line when it opened on 1 May 1979.

St John's Wood

This is the Underground station for Abbey Road where the Beatles recording studios were. At this station there is a Beatles-themed coffee shop.

Baker Street, Bond Street and Green Park

These stations have a common style from when the line opened in 1979.

Westminster

Westminster station had to be constructed underneath the 19th century District and Circle lines. The escalator hall is a thirty-metre deep concrete box full of escalators and stairs and enclosed in steel tubes. Michael Hopkins and Partners were the architects.

Waterloo

Waterloo is the second busiest Underground station on the network. It is one of two underground stations with a moving walkway. The other is Bank.

Southwark

Southwark Underground station was opened on 20 November 1999 as part of the Jubilee line extension. The station was designed by Sir Richard MacCormac of MJP Architects. The curving wall here is lined with patterned blue glass by artist Alex Beleschenko.

London Bridge

London Bridge station opened on 7 October 1999 as part of the Jubilee line extension. It is the only station on the Underground with the word "London" in its name.

Bermondsey

The station was opened on 17 September 1999 and the station was designed by Ian Ritchie Architects.

Canada Water

Another station with wide island platforms.

Canary Wharf

This enormous station is the only one on the Underground to be designed by Sir Norman Foster. It also has the widest 'island' platform of any Underground station.

The construction of Canary Wharf Underground station was partially funded by the Canary Wharf developers.

North Greenwich

North Greenwich Underground station is the one which serves the O2 Arena.

Canning Town

The Jubilee line comes into the open just before it reaches Canning Town. The Jubilee line here runs alongside the Docklands Light Railway.

West Ham

West Ham is an important interchange station with other lines.

Stratford

Stratford is the largest interchange station outside London.

METROPOLITAN LINE

The Metropolitan line started as the Metropolitan Railway company and London's first underground railway had seven stations from Paddington to Farringdon.

Amersham

If you stand on this footbridge at Amersham you are at the highest possible point that you can be on the Underground system.

Chesham

There is an old signal box and water tower at Chesham Underground station. It is also a Grade II Listed Building.

Chalfont & Latimer

A four-car shuttle train once ran from here to Chesham.

Chorleywood

When the station opened in 1889 it was known as "Chorley Wood" and was then called "Chorley Wood and Chenies" for a while.

On the northbound platform at Chorleywood there is a disused signal box that has been painted in Metropolitan Railway colours.

Rickmansworth

There is a water tower at the north end of the southbound platform. Rickmansworth was, until 1961, the changeover point between electric and steam-hauled trains.

Moor Park

There is track here that allows trains to get onto the Watford branch without going down to Moor Park.

Croxley

At this station there is a gallery of photographs of the Metropolitan line in olden days.

Watford

Watford is another Grade II Listed Building by Metropolitan Railway architect Charles Walter Clark.

Northwood

The station you would have seen in the 1970's TV Series 'The Good Life.'

Northwood Hills

Northwood Hills Underground station opened on 13 November 1933 and is between Northwood and Pinner on the Metropolitan line.

Pinner

The station remained the terminus of the Metropolitan Railway until 1 September 1887 when the line was extended to Rickmansworth. The station was also, until the 1960's, served by Great Central mainline trains.

North Harrow

Last on the Metropolitan line to retain the original wooden shelters from when it opened.

North Harrow station was rebuilt in the 1930's.

Harrow-on-the-Hill Underground station.

Northwick Park

Northwick Park and Kenton station are very close together.

Preston Road

Originally named Preston Road Halt for Uxendon and Kenton. A replacement station was built in 1931.

Wembley Park

The station has six London Underground tracks, with the two Jubilee line tracks in the centre flanked by slow and fast Metropolitan line tracks.

Finchley Road

Between Finchley Road and Baker Street, the first daylight stretch is a former station at Marlborough Road.

Baker Street

Over the top of Baker Street station is a block of flats known as Chiltern Court. Completed in 1929 and by architect Charles Walter Clark, its the largest residential block above an Underground Station.

West Harrow

It is the only station on the Uxbridge branch to be served exclusively by the Metropolitan line.

Rayners Lane

Rayners Lane opened as Rayners Lane Halt on 26 May 1906. The station was rebuilt in the 1930's to a design by Charles Holden.

Eastcote

Platforms at Eastcote have some of the nicest flowers and flowerbeds you will see at any station on the Underground.

Ruislip Manor

High up on the wall of the ticket hall is an old clock.

Ruislip

There is an old signal box at the eastern end of Ruislip station.

Ickenham

The original electrical sub-station is still in use today.

Hillingdon

Hillingdon station had to be re-sited from its original location when the A40 road was widened.

Uxbridge

One of the most decorative stations on the Metropolitan line. Designed by Charles Holden there are stained glass windows, preserved cigarette vending machines and a superb clock.

UNDERGROUND
UXBRIDGE STATION
METROPOLITAN LINE
PICCADILLY LINE

NORTHERN LINE

The Northern line was built as two separate railway companies – the 'Hampstead Tube' and the City & South London Railway. They merged to form what is now the Northern line.

Morden

Morden was where 'park and ride' started in 1926 when the station opened.

South Wimbledon

On the southbound platform is a name sign that says 'South Wimbledon [Merton] on it.

Colliers Wood

Exit the station and over the road is a pub called 'The Charles Holden' named after the architect who designed many Underground stations.

Tooting Broadway and Tooting Bec

Two more Charles Holden designed stations, Tooting Broadway featured in the TV Series 'Citizen Smith'.

Below, uplighters at Tooting Broadway.

Balham

Balham station opened on 6 December 1926 as part of the Morden extension.

Clapham South

Clapham South is one of several locations on the Northern line where deep-level shelters were built to be used during the Second World War.

Clapham Common

Clapham Common and nearby Clapham North stations are the only ones remaining on the Underground with narrow, island platforms.

Clapham Common station has a domed roof and a 'To The Trains' sign.

Clapham North

Clapham North like Clapham Common has a narrow, island platform that is only 14 feet in width. Angel and Euston used to have similar island platforms until they were upgraded.

Stockwell

Stockwell is another of several London Underground stations with adjacent deep-level air-raid shelters. The original building here was by Thomas Phillips Figgis.

Oval

Open on 18 December 1890 as part of the City and South London Railway.

Kennington

Kennington also has a domed roof like Clapham Common station.

Waterloo and Embankment

From Waterloo you can take the Bakerloo line for one station.

Charing Cross

A lot of TV filming takes place at Charing Cross.

Leicester Square

On the original Leslie Green station for the Piccadilly line there is evidence it was used by the publishers of Wisden Cricketers' Almanac

Tottenham Court Road

Like the Central line, Northern line platforms have some tiles with Eduardo Paolozzi's artwork.

Goodge Street

Opened on 22 June 1907 as Tottenham Court Road but changed its name to Goodge Street on 9 March 1908.

Warren Street

Go to the back end of the southbound platform and you will see that the station's original name was Euston Road.

Euston

The Northern line here had narrow island platforms like Clapham North and Clapham Common but they were widened when the Victoria line was built.

King's Cross St Pancras

Victoria line platforms at King's Cross St Pancras have a tiled motif in the seat recesses designed by artist Tom Eckersley. This is the busiest station on the network.

Angel

Angel has the longest escalator on the whole of the system. The three escalators with a 27.4 metre rise were brought into use in 1992 when the station was rebuilt. It has an extra wide south bound platform.

Old Street

The station was opened on 17 November 1901 as an extension of the City and South London Railway. It was part of the extension from Moorgate to Angel. The Northern City line platforms were opened on 14 February 1904 by the Great Northern & City Railway.

Borough

Opened on 18 December 1890 as part of the first deep-level tube railway, the City and South London Railway.

Mornington Crescent

The station's name was made famous by the BBC Radio 4 programme "I'm sorry I haven't a clue." The programmes host - Willie Rushton - has a plaque with his name in the ticket office.

Regular members of the Radio 4 comedy were Willie Rushton, Humphrey Lyttelton, Barry Cryer, Tim Brooke-Taylor and Graeme Garden.

Camden Town

The station was opened on 22 June 1907 by David Lloyd George who at the time was President of the Board of Trade.

Edgware

The station was opened on 18 August 1924 as an extension of the Charing Cross, Euston & Hampstead Railway. It was designed by architect Stanley Heaps.

Burnt Oak to Brent Cross

Burnt Oak, Hendon Central and Brent Cross all have a chessboard pattern on the floors of their booking halls.

Golders Green

Platform 1 is only used by train crew.

Hampstead

Hampstead is the deepest station on the network. There is lettering in the tilework that says 'Heath Street' a name the station was going to be called before it opened as Hampstead.

Belsize Park

Belsize Park is a Grade II Listed Building.

Belsize Park is another station on the Northern line with wartime deep-level shelters. Like Chalk Farm the building was designed by Leslie Green.

Chalk Farm Underground station.

Chalk Farm has the shallowest lifts on the Northern line. The Leslie Green building also has the longest frontage of any station.

High Barnet, Totteridge & Whetstone and Woodside Park

These stations were opened on 1 April 1872 by the Great Northern Railway.

West Finchley

The station was opened on 1 March 1933 by the London & North Eastern Railway.

Mill Hill East

The station, originally named Mill Hill, opened on 22 August 1867.

Finchley Central

Harry Beck who designed the original Underground map lived in Finchley. On the Southbound platform is a reproduction of his original 1933 map.

East Finchley

From the southern end of the platforms you can see 'The Archer' a three metre tall statue by artist Eric Aumonier.

Highgate

Underground platforms at Highgate are longer as they were designed for trains of nine carriages.

Archway

This station was originally called Highgate. When the station we now know as Highgate was built this station became 'Archway.'

Tufnell Park

Tufnell Park is one of the lesser-used stations on this part of the Northern line.

Kentish Town

The station was designed by Leslie Green as can be seen from its ox-blood red terracota facade. When Kentish Town opened, the next Charing Cross, Euston and Hampstead Railway south was South Kentish Town. That station closed in 1924 due to low usage, but the building remains.

PICCADILLY LINE

The Piccadilly line started as the Great Northern, Piccadilly & Brompton Railway running from Finsbury Park.

In the 1930's the Piccadilly line was extended at both ends and many of these stations were designed by architect Charles Holden.

Heathrow Terminal Stations

Heathrow Terminal 4, like Chesham, Mill Hill East and Kensington (Olympia), has just one platform. Travel between the different Heathrow stations is free.

Hatton Cross

Hatton Cross station opened in 1975.

Hounslow West

The station was originally known as Hounslow Barracks when it opened.

Hounslow Central

Hounslow Central, originally named Heston & Hounslow opened on 1 April 1886.

Hounslow East

This station was designed by Acanthus Lawrence Wrightson Architects.

Osterley

There was a previous station building from when the station was known as 'Osterley Park and Spring Grove.' It is now a bookshop. Osterley and Spring Grove opened on 1st May 1883 and was resited on 25th March 1934.

Boston Manor

The only station to have appeared on British postage stamps in January 2013.

Northfields

The station opened as Northfield (Ealing) on 16 April 1908 and was then renamed Northfields and Little Ealing on 11 December 1911. It is currently a Grade II Listed Building.

South Ealing

Piccadilly line services began running through South Ealing from 29 April 1935.

South Harrow

Opened on 28 June 1903 by the District Railway. The original and now disused station building for South Harrow can be seen at the southern end of the southbound platform.

Sudbury Hill

The original station opened on 28 June 1903 by the Metropolitan District Railway.

It was rebuilt by architects Adams, Holden & Pearson in preparation for the transfer of services to the Piccadilly line on 4 July 1932.

Sudbury Town

Sudbury Town has a barometer inside the station and the original wooden free-standing ticket office (passimeter) is still there.

Alperton

At one time Alperton station had an escalator going up to platform level.

Park Royal

Park Royal is not a Charles Holden designed station. The architects were Herbert Welch and Felix Lander.

North Ealing

This station was opened on 23 June 1903 by the District Railway. A 1930's railway sub-station is built alongside the Eastbound platform.

Ealing Common

Opened on 1 July 1879 by the District Railway, the station was known as Ealing Common and West Acton from 1886 to 1910.

Hammersmith

Hammersmith station is part of a rebuilt shopping centre.

Barons Court

The station was built 1905 – the year when the District Railway opened the station. The Piccadilly line opened the following year.

There are green tiles in the ticket hall and wooden benches on the platforms at Barons Court.

Earl's Court

Escalators were introduced here in 1911 to link the Piccadilly and District line platforms.

Gloucester Road

Two station buildings next to one another, the original Leslie Green building now occupied by shops.

Knightsbridge

One exit was built to be right next to Harrods. It is also the nearest station for the Oriental Mandarin Hotel.

Hyde Park Corner

As you are heading east from Hyde Park Corner on the right hand side will be the disused Down Street station.

Green Park

Green Park station is a Grade II Listed Building.

Piccadilly Circus

There is a World Clock here showing times in different zones. It is also the nearest station for the Criterion Theatre.

Leicester Square

The distance between Leicester Square and Covent Garden, the next station, is one of the shortest on the Underground.

Covent Garden

In the past there have been proposals to close Covent Garden station. There is an old style roundel at the front end of the westbound platform and other period signage such as "TO THE LIFTS & STAIRS"

"TO THE TRAINS" signs at Covent Garden.

Above, an illuminated "LIFT TO STREET" sign at Covent Garden just outside the lifts.

Holborn

Holborn has four platforms. Two for the Central line and two for the Piccadilly line.

There are two more abandoned platforms that were once used for a shuttle down to Aldwych. It closed in 1994.

Russell Square

Another Leslie Green designed station and another Grade II Listed Building.

King's Cross St. Pancras

The most complicated station on the network and the busiest.

Caledonian Road and Holloway Road

Caledonian Road has a name sign in the original 1908 style. Both Caledonian Road and Holloway Road are Leslie W. Green designed buildings.

Arsenal

This station was known as "Gillespie Road" until it was renamed Arsenal in 1932. Evidence of this can still be seen in the tile work.

Finsbury Park

The Great Northern, Piccadilly and Brompton Railway (now London Underground's Piccadilly line) opened on 15 December 1906 between Finsbury Park and Hammersmith.

Manor House, Turnpike Lane, Wood Green, Bounds Green

The section from Finsbury Park to Cockfosters was built as an extension to the line in the 1930's. The architect was Charles Holden.

Arnos Grove

Arnos Grove is a Grade II* Listed Building. In the middle of the ticket hall is an exhibition all about architect Charles Holden.

Southgate

Southgate is another Charles Holden designed station and another Grade II Listed Building.

Oakwood

Oakwood – the second most northerly station on the Piccadilly line was called Enfield West when it opened on 13 March 1933. On 3 May 1934 it was renamed Enfield West (Oakwood) and then on 1 September 1946 it was renamed Oakwood.

Cockfosters

Cockfosters station is the northern terminus of the Piccadilly line. The station opened on 31 July 1933 some four months after neighbouring Oakwood. Again a station designed by Charles Holden and a Grade II Listed Building.

Bus information

TICKETS
AND
INFORMATION
TRAINS

VICTORIA LINE

The Victoria line was opened between 1968 and 1971 in different stages. Every station has its own unique platform tiling 'motif.'

Brixton

The roundel over the entrance is one of the largest on the underground and there is a superb artist's drawing.

Stockwell

Across the street from Stockwell Underground station is 'The Swan' pub.

Vauxhall

The Victoria line was extended from Victoria to Brixton and the station was opened on 23 July 1971.

Pimlico

At Pimlico there is another Underground roundel etched into the concrete below.

Victoria

Victoria Underground station is the fourth busiest station on the network and is served by the District, Circle and Victoria lines.

Green Park

The station was opened by the Great Northern, Piccadilly and Brompton Railway on 15 December 1906 and was originally named Dover Street. It is the nearest station for the Ritz Hotel.

Oxford Circus

Oxford Circus is the station where Bakerloo, Central and Victoria lines all intersect.

Warren Street

In 1934 the current existing station building replaced the original when escalators were installed. The Victoria line platforms opened on 1 December 1968.

Euston

Euston was originally constructed as two separate Underground stations. Euston is not served by Circle, Hammersmith & City and Metropolitan lines. Nearby Euston Square is served by these lines.

King's Cross St Pancras

There is a plaque here remembering those who lost their lives in the 1987 King's Cross Underground fire.

Highbury & Islington

Across the road from the current entrance is the 1904 building of the Great Northern & City Railway Highbury & Islington station.

Finsbury Park

This station was not built by the Underground but by the main line railway.

Seven Sisters

Most Victoria line trains use platforms 3 and 5. Platform 4 is often used for terminating trains going to the depot at Northumberland Park.

Tottenham Hale

Tottenham Hale is a National Rail and London Underground interchange. The station opened in 1840 with Underground services added in 1968.

Blackhorse Road

Another joint London Overground and London underground station. As well as being on the Victoria line of the Underground it is also on the Gospel Oak to Barking line of the London Overground.

Walthamstow Central

The original plan had been for the Victoria line to terminate at Wood Street, one station beyond Walthamstow Central.

WATERLOO & CITY LINE

Opened in 1898, the Underground Line that is two stops – Bank and Waterloo – did not become part of the Underground until 1994.

South Kentish Town

South Kentish Town was situated on the Charing Cross Euston & Hampstead Railway between stations at Camden Town and Kentish Town. It opened on 22 June 1907 and closed on 5 June 1924. The street level building designed by Leslie W. Green was on the west side of Kentish Town Road.

Originally it had been intended that the station would be known as Castle Road and this name was included in platform tunnel tiling.

The street level building has been used for commercial purposes since closure and has served as a Motorcycle shop and as a Cash Converters shop.

Down Street

The station at Down Street, situated between Dover Street (Green Park) and Hyde Park Corner stations on the Great Northern Piccadilly & Brompton Railway. It opened on 15 March 1907 and closed on 22 May 1932.

The surface building was designed by Leslie W. Green and was on the south-west side of Down Street. Down Street was little used - it was just over five hundred yards from Hyde Park Corner and just over six hundred yards from Dover Street.

York Road

York Road was opened by the Great Northern Piccadilly & Brompton Railway on 15th December 1906 and was situated between King's Cross station and Caledonian Road station.

The street level building, by architect Leslie W. Green, was at the corner of York Way and Bingfield Street. The glazed ruby-red tiling was by the Leeds Fireclay Company.

After closure in 1932 the raised lettering on the frieze was chiselled off for subsequent lessees.

Brompton Road

Brompton Road was opened by the Great Northern, Piccadilly & Brompton Railway on 15th December 1906. The street level building, designed by Leslie W. Green, occupied an L-shaped site facing both Brompton Road and Cottage Place. The station was particularly convenient for getting to the Brompton Oratory and the Victoria & Albert Museum but the station was very close to both South Kensington station and Knightsbridge station. These stations proved to be more popular. The street level building was sold to HM Commissioners of Crown Lands on 4th November 1938, having been closed since 30th July 1934.

Marlborough Road

Marlborough Road was opened on 13th April 1868 by the Metropolitan & Saint John's Wood Railway, and the street level building stood at the corner of Finchley Road and Queen's Grove.

With the Bakerloo line being extended from Baker Street to Finchley Road and with a new tube station at St. John's Wood, the station at Marlborough Road closed on 20th November 1939.

Aldwych

Aldwych station opened as Strand on 30th November 1907 before being renamed Aldwych on 9th May 1915. The station was designed by Leslie W. Green and had entrances on both the Strand and in Surrey Street.

Aldwych station was temporarily closed from 22nd September 1940 to 1st July 1946 before finally closing on the 3rd October 1994.